TWISTED JOURNEYS® #12

Kung Fu Masters

Evonne Tsang

Illustrated by Alitha E Martinez

LERNER   APOLIS

Story by Evonne Tsang

Pencils and inks by Alitha E. Martinez

Colouring by Hi-Fi Design

Lettering by Marshall Dillon

Graphic Universe™ is a trademark and Twisted Journeys® is a registered trademark of Lerner Publishing Group, Inc.

First published in the United Kingdom in 2010 by
Lerner Books,
Dalton House,
60 Windsor Avenue,
London SW19 2RR

Website address: www.lernerbooks.co.uk

This edition updated for UK publication in 2010

A CIP catalogue record for this title is available from the British Library

ISBN-13: 978 0 7613 5405 5

Printed in China

ARE YOU READY FOR YOUR *Twisted Journeys®?* ***YOU*** ARE THE HERO OF THE BOOK YOU'RE ABOUT TO READ. YOUR JOURNEYS WILL BE PACKED WITH ADVENTURES FIGHTING BANDITS, GHOSTS, AND DANGEROUS RIVALS. AND EVERY STORY STARS ***YOU!***

EACH PAGE TELLS WHAT HAPPENS TO ***YOU*** AS YOU TRAVEL TO CHINA TO BECOME A MASTER OF KUNG FU. ***YOUR*** WORDS AND THOUGHTS ARE SHOWN IN THE ***YELLOW BALLOONS***. AND YOU GET TO DECIDE WHAT HAPPENS NEXT. JUST FOLLOW THE NOTE AT THE BOTTOM OF EACH PAGE UNTIL YOU REACH A *Twisted Journeys®* PAGE. THEN MAKE THE CHOICE ***YOU*** LIKE BEST.

BUT BE CAREFUL... THE WRONG CHOICE COULD BRING YOUR TRAVELS TO A VERY QUICK END!

The Middle Kingdom may be the most powerful empire in the world, but your corner of it is pretty boring. You do the same things every day. After morning lessons with your tutor and some lunch, you help your parents. They run an apothecary shop in part of your home.

The shop walls are covered with tiny drawers full of dried herbs and preserved animal parts. Your parents prescribe these as medicine for their patients. You're tired of the medicine's bitter smell, which gets into your clothes and fills the house.

You sweep the shop, serve tea to patients, and wrap prescriptions in paper packets tied with string. You've poured so many cups of tea that you have nightmares about pouring endless cups of tea to an endless line of patients.

Every once in a long while, your father teaches you some *batgua kuen* kung fu. You want to learn more, but he thinks you're too young for real training. It's not fair, but there's nothing you can do about it.

TURN TO PAGE 28.

TWISTED JOURNEYS®

Those dumplings look pretty good, and you have
just enough money to pay for them, but it might
be a good idea to save your silver.

WILL YOU . . .

. . . agree to do some work for
free food and lodgings?
TURN TO PAGE 100.

. . . say that you have some silver
and can pay instead?
TURN TO PAGE 85.

Wahnsyu looks alarmed and says, "I hope that's not the cat I've seen hanging around here. Cats aggravate *geungsi*. We'll need to be careful."

He bars the shed door and quickly gathers his tools. He gets his coin sword, made from ancient coins bound with red string, and some extra *fu* spells.

He hands you an eight-sided mirror and says, "*Geungsi* are repulsed by their own reflection. Use this if one of them gets near you. Remember, they can't detect you if you hold your breath."

You protest that you don't want to get near the *geungsi* at all. But Wahnsyu points out that if he doesn't keep them under control, they'll attack the town. You admit it's better to help him before things get out of control.

He unbars the door, and the two of you cautiously enter the shed. The *geungsi* are agitated and are hopping in place. *Thump. Thump. Thump.* The noise fills the shed.

You clutch the mirror and search to the right while Wahnsyu goes left. You see the cat under a chair!

GO ON TO THE NEXT PAGE.

You need to get the cat out fast!

WILL YOU . . .

. . . grab the cat before it runs
somewhere else?
TURN TO PAGE 104.

. . . try to coax the cat
into your arms?
TURN TO PAGE 94.

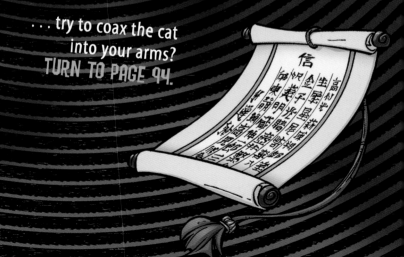

You say, "I saw Saamgo betraying everyone to the Black Serpent Society!"

Sun Simjam's eyes widen. She stares a moment and then says, "You must tell the others." You nod and start to walk past her. But suddenly you feel a sharp pain at the back of your neck.

You try to reach up to touch it, but your arm feels too heavy to lift. You see Sun Simjam replacing a pin in her hair. Your legs lose all strength, and you fall to the ground. You're awake, but you can't move!

Sun Simjam pushes your eyelids closed and says, "We can't have you giving everything away now." She carries you back to the others and tells them you have a fever and need bed rest.

Hours pass. Fa May checks on you but thinks you're sleeping. You eventually manage to open your eyes. If you try hard, you can twitch your fingers . . .

You hear swords clashing. The attack has begun! Even worse, you smell smoke and soon see the orange glow of fire through the windows. You struggle to move, but it's useless.

GO ON TO THE NEXT PAGE.

You hear the crackle of flames and realize that the fire has reached your room. You still can't move, and you seriously think you're going to die. Then your door crashes open. Fa May, covered in soot and injuries, runs in and throws you over her shoulder.

Fa May fights her way out through masked invaders and finally gets away. She reaches a cliff overlooking the mansion and puts you down. She asks, "Are you all right?"

Your mouth feels like it's full of sticky rice, and you sound funny, but you manage to say, "Yes, *sifu*."

The two of you watch the fire devour the mansion. Only Wu Waanfo manages to escape and find you. Everything and everyone else is consumed by the raging fire.

Two days later, Fa May ignores her injuries and defeats Duhkseh in their duel. It's been won at too high a cost, however. You, Fa May, and Wu Waanfo are a grim trio as you walk away from the bitter victory.

THE END

You get a wild idea. You *can* be like them! You can learn kung fu and have adventures all over the world! You just need to get one of them to accept you as a student.

Your parents would never let you do this, so you can't reveal who you really are. You'll have to say that you're an orphan. Your parents will be really worried if you just disappear, so you'll write them a letter once you're far away. You hope that they'll understand and forgive you.

The woman seems easygoing and cheerful, and you think it'll be easier to convince her to teach you. You don't know what style she practices. The monk looks like a Shaolin monk, and Shaolin kung fu is famous for its power. Either way, you'll finally get real training.

As you think about it, they finish eating, get up, and bow to each other. They begin to walk away.

You'd better decide which kung fu master you want to be your teacher! The woman is walking quickly down the road, but the monk is still nearby.

WILL YOU . . .

. . . talk to the Shaolin monk, though he may need more convincing?
TURN TO PAGE 54.

. . . try to catch up with the cheerful woman?
TURN TO PAGE 66.

MARSHAL GAO'S FORCES ATTACK LIANGSHAN MARSH, AND THE OUTLAWS SPRING INTO ACTION. YOU SERVE AS SONG JIANG'S PAGE.

THE OUTLAWS, PRETENDING TO PANIC, DRAW MARSHAL GAO DEEPER INTO LIANGSHAN MARSH.

NEXT, THE OUTLAWS SABOTAGE THE PADDLEBOATS TO TRAP THEM.

WE'VE CAPTURED MARSHAL GAO!

HURRAH!

I PROMISE TO ASK THE EMPEROR TO PARDON ALL THE OUTLAWS!

OUR GREATEST WISH IS TO SERVE THE EMPEROR. THANK YOU!

Song Jiang politely sends Marshal Gao on his way. Then Song Jiang sighs and says, "He won't help us. He's the most corrupt official of all. He is why most of us were forced to become outlaws."

You ask him why he let Marshal Gao go, and he says it is so that the emperor can see that the outlaws are honourable. He secretly sends men to ask the emperor for a pardon for their crimes.

Liangshan Marsh is quiet while everyone waits for news. The men finally return and report that Marshal Gao did not do what he promised. But they did meet with the emperor.

A few days later, Marshal Su arrives with the emperor's pardon. He also invites the outlaws to work for the emperor. Song Jiang and the outlaws are overjoyed and readily agree.

You get an official letter thanking you for your service and also an escort home. The historic event inspires you for the rest of your life. You never forget the outlaws of Liangshan Marsh.

THE END

You carefully follow Saamgo to a part of the house that looks older and unused. He enters an overgrown garden, and you're about to follow when a masked man dressed in black appears. You crouch by the doorway and listen.

The masked man says, "You're late."

"Complain later," Saamgo replies. "Fa May got the Hawk Wing Sabre repaired."

You risk a peek and see the masked man grab Saamgo's arm in shock. The masked man is wearing a ring shaped like a snake with two ruby eyes. He's from the Black Serpent Society!

The man says, "We'll make our move tonight. Take care of the guards with this." He hands Saamgo a paper packet like the ones your parents use in their shop. It's probably poison! The herbs that heal people can also be used to harm them.

You tiptoe away from the door and hurry toward the moon-viewing pavilion.

You run into Sun Simjam and are about to tell her everything. But then caution kicks in.

TWISTED JOURNEYS®

It's important to stop Saamgo as soon
as possible, but Fa May is the only
person you really know here.

WILL YOU . . .

. . . hurry and tell Sun Simjam
everything you saw?
TURN TO PAGE 9.

. . . wait and tell Fa May?
TURN TO PAGE 57.

Wahnsyu doesn't seem worried, so you follow him back into the shed.

It takes a moment for your eyes to adjust to the darkness, and you bump up against a chair. As it falls over, you feel something brush your leg, and you yell out.

Wahnsyu asks what happened. You tell him, but he shrugs. He says, "It was probably a rat. Lots of them in these old places."

You protest, "It was too big. Maybe it was the cat I saw before?"

Wahnsyu looks alarmed. "Cats agitate my clients!"

In fact, the *geungsi* have started shuddering. The cat must be near them!

Wahnsyu sees the cat on a shelf and tries to grab it, but it leaps onto a *geungsi*, knocking the fu off! Wahnsyu doesn't notice—he's chasing the cat.

You run for the exit, but the *geungsi* blocks you. You remember then to hold your breath, but it's too late to hide! The *geungsi* grabs you around the neck with its strong grip.

You struggle, but it's . . .

THE END

The bandits demand that you tell them who will pay your ransom money.

WILL YOU . . .

. . . tell them where you live, so your parents can pay the ransom and get you out of this mess?
TURN TO PAGE 65.

. . . take a wild chance and ask to join the bandits?
TURN TO PAGE 30.

. . . say nothing now and look for a chance to escape later?
TURN TO PAGE 36.

Sister Gau takes you out to a courtyard filled with kids practising kung fu in groups led by monks.

A monk bows to Sister Gau. She tells him, "Brother Houyi, I have a new student for you." She looks around and says, "The children seem to be working hard."

"They're excited about the demonstration," he says.

Sister Gau nods. "It could be a great chance for one of them." She sees your questioning look and explains, "*Sifu* Mohdihkge, Shaolin's most talented hero, is looking for his first apprentice. The children hope he will choose one of them when he sees them at the demonstration."

Some of the kids have noticed you. You're a little nervous. You've known everyone back home your whole life. You've never had to meet so many strangers at once.

Sister Gau signals to one of the monks, who sends a boy over. The boy bows to Sister Gau and greets her with, "*Sifu*." He's older than you and has a shaved head like the monks.

GO ON TO THE NEXT PAGE.

Sister Gau says, "Noiheung, would you introduce our new student to the other children?" He nods, and Sister Gau takes her leave of you.

Brother Houyi says, "Practice is almost over, so you can just watch for today. I need to return to my students."

Noiheung points out a few of the exercises until training ends. Then the students relax and find their friends for conversation and games.

You see two groups of kids walking toward you, and Noiheung says, "Here they come."

One group is led by a big boy who walks with a swagger. Their clothes are old, with repairs and torn edges.

Noiheung explains, "That boy is Juklaam. Like me, he and his friends are temple orphans. The other group is Gasi's. Their families are mostly merchants."

Gasi's group has new clothes, and Gasi has a grown-up hairstyle. They keep throwing looks of disgust at Juklaam. The temple orphans sneer back at the merchant kids.

GO ON TO THE NEXT PAGE.

TWISTED JOURNEYS®

They're really pushing you to take a side.

WILL YOU . . .

. . . admit that you have parents
and join the merchant kids?

TURN TO PAGE 60.

. . . stick with the story that you're an
orphan and join the temple kids?

TURN TO PAGE 26.

. . . try to stay neutral like
Noiheung and not take sides?

TURN TO PAGE 88.

You grab onto your father and say, "It's too dangerous!"

Seeing how upset you are, your mother says, "I'm sure everyone saw the magistrate's notice and they're all being careful." Your father reluctantly agrees to stay.

Your family huddles together in the room all night. Although nothing happens, you're glad when dawn comes.

The three of you go out to check on the town. A few people stand in the street talking about the *geungsi* attack.

There are some houses with smashed-in doors. You feel guilty, but you're glad your parents are safe.

Your family sleeps during the day, expecting another attack after sunset. The night seems quiet at first. Then you hear noises at your neighbour's house.

Soon it's the doors and windows of your own home getting smashed in. The priest's *geungsi* and townspeople who have become *geungsi* have combined into a group large enough to break through your protections!

You and your parents fight . . . but you're overwhelmed and fall to the *geungsi*.

THE END

You leave the road and walk through the dry autumn grass toward the inn. The late afternoon sun casts a golden light upon Windy Hill. The brittle grass rustles as you walk through it. A quieter rustle turns out to be a cat slinking about on mysterious cat business.

As you get closer to the inn, you see a man wearing the yellow robes and folded black hat of a Taoist priest. He looks young, with a sturdy square face and a scraggly little beard.

He sees you and waves. "Hello! I didn't think anyone would be willing to come up here."

That sounds weird. You say, "Hello. Why not?"

He looks surprised. "Don't you know why I'm here? I thought it was all arranged with the local magistrate. My name's Wahnsyu."

You say you haven't heard anything about him, and he explains. "I'm transporting clients back to their hometowns up north for burial."

TURN TO PAGE 71.

Even though your father thinks you're too young, you know there are lots of kung fu schools full of kids your age. Those kids aren't stuck in a shop in a small town, either.

At least you get to go out today. Your mother asks you to deliver a prescription to an old woman who lives far outside of town. The old woman thanks you for the delivery with some extra coins. You walk along the dusty road, thinking about getting some buns and a nice cup of tea at the roadside tea shop. But up ahead, you see something strange.

It looks like someone is at the abandoned inn on Windy Hill. You squint hard in that direction, but the sun is in your eyes, and you can't see much. You wonder why someone would go up there and if they know the inn is closed.

GO ON TO THE NEXT PAGE.

WILL YOU . . .

. . . go up the hill and check out
the abandoned inn?
TURN TO PAGE 27.

. . . continue to the tea shop for
your snack and a break?
TURN TO PAGE 11.

"Wait!" you shout, thinking fast. You once heard your parents talking about outlaws based in Liangshan Marsh. They were victims of corrupt officials and not really evil. You hope these guys are those outlaws. "Are you the heroic outlaws of Liangshan Marsh? I'm here to join you!"

The bandits look surprised. Their leader asks, "How can a scrawny kid like you help? You're just another mouth to feed."

"I know *batgua kuen*," you exaggerate.

The leader grins. "Well, maybe we can use you. I'm Mahjeuk. Welcome to the gang."

You sigh in relief. A few of the outlaws grumble about losing the ransom money, but they seem willing to accept you.

Mahjeuk says, "Put the woman's sword where she can reach it to cut herself free when she wakes up. We should go before anyone sees us. Let's be careful to cover our tracks and not leave a trail."

You follow the outlaws off the road into the woods.

30

TURN TO PAGE 39.

Even though the *sehjing*, or snake spirit, didn't seem dangerous, you'd rather not take any risks. She doesn't chase you, and soon you're back to where you were: alone and lost in a dark forest.

You wonder if you're far enough away to risk calling out again when a big, dark shape drops out of a tree in front of you. The shape says in Brother Wo's voice, "It's just me! I've finally found you!"

You're so relieved that you almost cry. You can't seem to stop babbling. "There was a giant bear and then these stinging bugs and this stupid squirrel! Then it was dark, and a *sehjing* showed up—"

Brother Wo interrupts you, asking, "You saw a *sehjing*? Where?"

He seems pretty upset, so you try to reassure him. "She seemed pretty harmless, actually, but it was so weird—"

"*Sehjing* are dangerous! They must be trapped whenever you see one! Did it try to lure you into its home? Where did you see it?"

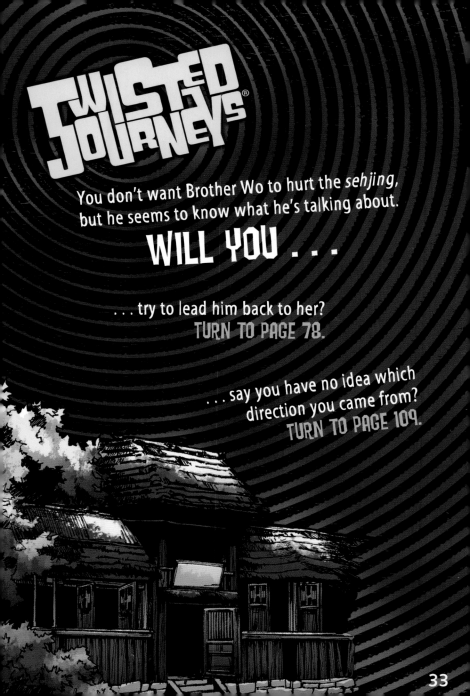

TWISTED JOURNEYS®

You don't want Brother Wo to hurt the *sehjing*, but he seems to know what he's talking about.

WILL YOU . . .

. . . try to lead him back to her?
TURN TO PAGE 78.

. . . say you have no idea which direction you came from?
TURN TO PAGE 109.

SISTER GAU IS PRETTY UNDERSTANDING WHEN YOU EXPLAIN YOU WANT TO LEAVE. SHE ASKS ANOTHER NUN TO TAKE YOU HOME.

WE'VE BEEN SO WORRIED ABOUT YOU!

WE WERE AFRAID THAT BANDITS KIDNAPPED YOU!

BUT NO ONE ASKED FOR RANSOM, AND WE FEARED THE WORST!

WE'RE GLAD YOU'RE SAFE, BUT YOU'RE IN BIG TROUBLE.

YOU'LL SPEND THE NEXT THREE MONTHS COPYING CONFUCIUS'S LESSONS ABOUT THE IMPORTANCE OF OBEYING AND RESPECTING YOUR PARENTS.

ALTHOUGH THE COPYING IS VERY LONG AND VERY BORING, YOU DON'T REALLY MIND...

...SINCE YOUR MORNINGS ARE NOW MUCH BETTER-- TRAINING WITH YOUR FATHER EVERY DAY!

THE END

34

You forget about Saamgo. The Shining Hawk warriors celebrate until late into the night.

Fa May shows you to a room, where you tumble into bed and fall asleep.

You are woken up by a hand over your face and realize you're being bound and gagged . . . by Saamgo! The outlaw carries you out to a masked man in black, who slings you over his shoulder.

The man walks an hour to a cave and lights a torch. You see his snake-shaped ring and realize that he's with the Black Serpent Society!

The man says, "Let's see how well Fa May duels when she realizes her dear student's gone." He throws you into a pit of snakes that go into a frenzy and attack you. Their poison works fast and kills you quickly.

Unfortunately, the plan works, and Fa May is distracted with worry. It's a duel to the death—and Duhkseh defeats her. Although Wu Waanfo immediately challenges and defeats Duhkseh, it is too late for you and Fa May.

THE END

GO ON TO THE NEXT PAGE.

You nod. You're stiff from being tied up for so long, so the monk helps you up.

Fa May says, "Brother Wo overheard some merchants talking about bandits attacking this road. He kindly came back to warn me."

You bow to Brother Wo and say, "Thank you for helping me, *sifu*."

He replies, "I'm of low rank. Please call me Brother Wo."

Fa May says to you, "I'm terribly sorry, but I'll need to use *hing kung*, light-body skill, to get to my duel in time. I can't take you."

You're kind of relieved. You've only been away from home for a day, and you've already been captured by bandits.

Fa May bows to Brother Wo and jumps into the trees, leaping through the branches as if she were lighter than air. You sigh and think that if you can learn a strong kung fu like hers, you won't need to fear bandits.

GO ON TO THE NEXT PAGE.

Brother Wo says that he can take you home or take you to the school at the Shaolin temple.

WILL YOU . . .

. . . go home?
TURN TO PAGE 50.

. . . travel to the Shaolin temple?
TURN TO PAGE 45.

You're confused when you arrive at an abandoned temple on a forested mountainside. It's not marshy at all!

Mahjeuk explains, "I might as well admit that we're not the Liangshan Marsh outlaws. We're actually the bandits of Leaping Deer Mountain."

He continues, "Honestly, we're not doing that well at being bandits. So we want to join the Liangshan Marsh outlaws. We heard that one of them, Li Kui, is in jail and condemned to death. If we rescue him, they'll let us join."

He sweeps an arm at his men and asks, "So, kid, be honest. What do we look like?"

You look at their ragged clothes and wild hair and say, "Um, bandits?"

Mahjeuk nods in agreement and says they need someone to scout who *doesn't* look like a bandit. It'll take two days to get to the town where Li Kui is being held. You'll go in and spy for them.

GO ON TO THE NEXT PAGE.

When you get to the town,
Mahjeuk gives you a few ounces of silver
and tells you to check out the jail.

WILL YOU . . .

. . . spy on the jail and report back to the bandits?
TURN TO PAGE 51.

. . . turn in the bandits to the authorities?
TURN TO PAGE 86.

. . . run away and use the silver to get home?
TURN TO PAGE 5.

You only know some very basic *batgua kuen*, but you hope it's enough. You stand with your legs apart so that you feel balanced. You're not strong enough to attack the bandit, but maybe—

You have no time to think as the bandit charges. You roll under the force of his attack and use his momentum to throw him onto his back. The bandit seems stunned. You did it!

You realize that the bandit could've grabbed you if he'd approached you calmly. Another bandit stares at his fallen comrade in disbelief and then turns toward you. You want him to charge without thinking too, so you sneer at him. "Can't even beat a kid? You must be the worst bandits in the world!"

The bandit roars, "You stinking brat! I'll tear you apart!"

As you hoped, he's so angry that he just charges. You feel surprisingly calm and ready for his attack.

GO ON TO THE NEXT PAGE.

You take a quick step forward and get under this bandit as well. You throw him over you, but then he grabs your leg. He isn't stunned! You try to jerk your leg out of his grip, but he easily hangs onto you.

The bandit smirks and starts to get up—then Fa May suddenly appears and knocks him out with her sword. You step away from him and look around. Fa May has defeated all the other bandits!

She says, "Good job."

"Thank you, *sifu*," you reply happily, glad that you stood up for yourself and impressed her.

Fa May says, "Well, let's get going. Wudang Mountain isn't getting any closer."

As you walk, Fa May asks about your training. She gives you exercises to practice, but she says that it will be hard to do real training on the road. You don't mind, since you are already learning more than your father ever showed you.

After a week of travel, you finally arrive at Wudang Mountain.

WUDANG MOUNTAIN

MARTIAL ARTISTS ARE A PART OF THE *GONGWU* BROTHERHOOD. *GONGWU,* WHICH MEANS "RIVER AND LAKE," IS THE WORLD OF THOSE WHO LIVE OUTSIDE NORMAL SOCIETY.

OUR LIFE IS ONE OF BOTH FREEDOM AND DANGER. NOTHING IS MORE IMPORTANT THAN HONOUR.

AS YOU KNOW, I'M MEETING SOMEONE FOR A DUEL.

SINCE YOU ARE NEW HERE, I DON'T WANT YOU TO FEEL YOU HAVE TO TAKE MY SIDE. I OFFER YOU A CHANCE TO REMAIN NEUTRAL.

IF YOU JOIN ME, MY ENEMIES WILL BECOME YOUR ENEMIES. IT CAN GET DANGEROUS.

GO ON TO THE NEXT PAGE.

TWISTED JOURNEYS®

Fa May has been nice to you, but it might be a good idea to avoid taking sides for now.

WILL YOU . . .

. . . play it safe and ask Fa May to introduce you to a neutral *sifu*?
TURN TO PAGE 69.

. . . stay loyal to Fa May and risk the dangers of taking her side?
TURN TO PAGE 90.

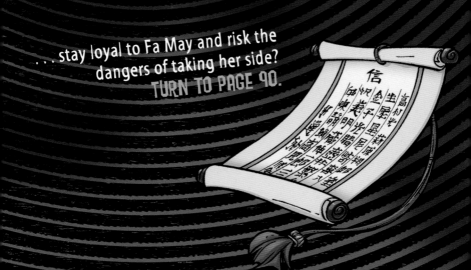

You decide that you're not ready to give up your adventuring yet! You tell Brother Wo that you want to go to the Shaolin temple.

The two of you travel through the moonlit mountain forest. The woods seem silent at first. But the longer you walk, the more you can hear animals rustling in the darkness, leaves whispering in the wind, and the *whoosh* of night birds overhead.

After a couple of hours, you're really tired. You fall farther and farther behind. Brother Wo notices and asks if you'd like to sleep.

You nod, thinking that you'll make camp. But Brother Wo kneels in front of you and tells you to climb on his back. You protest that you can walk a little farther.

"It's all right," Brother Wo says. "We'll move faster this way."

Too tired to argue any further, you get on his back. You fall asleep dreaming that you're a bird flying through a dark forest, gently rising and falling, covering great distances.

GO ON TO THE NEXT PAGE.

ON TO THE NEXT PAGE

Looking at you, Sister Gau says, "You seem like you've been through quite a lot. Would you like to get cleaned up and change your clothes?"

You notice that your clothes are a mess after travelling on a dusty road, getting tied up by bandits, and sleeping in what you're wearing. You don't smell so great, either.

You follow Sister Gau to the baths, where a young nun fills a tub with hot water. You bathe and put on the clean uniform left for you and then poke your head out of the room.

Sister Gau is helping the novice fold towels. Despite having only one arm, she folds faster than the novice. Her movements are fast and assured, and you realize that her kung fu is probably pretty powerful.

You stifle a yawn. Without turning her head, Sister Gau says, "Most of the students are in class now. Would you like to join them, or would you prefer to rest in your room and meet them later?"

GO ON TO THE NEXT PAGE.

WILL YOU . . .

. . . jump right in and go to class
immediately?
TURN TO PAGE 21.

. . . catch up on sleep first
and meet people later?
TURN TO PAGE 80.

You run back into the mansion, calling for help. You get lost and waste precious time until you run into Wu Waanfo.

You explain what happened, and he races for the garden faster than you can run. When you hear his cry of dismay, your heart sinks.

You hurry outside and see him holding Fa May's limp body. She has snakebites all over, and the snake is gone.

Wu Waanfo is furious. He rallies the Shining Hawk Association and their allies against the Black Serpent Society. You want to help, but you're told to stay out of the way.

Fa May doesn't die, but she will be an invalid, in bed for the rest of her life. No one will let you see her.

After the Black Serpent Society is destroyed, Wu Waanfo summons you. He says, "You abandoned your *sifu* to danger. You're too unworthy to be a warrior."

He condemns you to be a lowly servant, sweeping floors and carrying rubbish for the rest of your life.

THE END

Although you ran away, you are ready to go home. Your encounter with the bandits was more excitement than you expected. Brother Wo says, "Sometimes we must be foolish before we become wise. I'm sure your parents will be happy to have you home."

You walk several hours before bedding down for the night in the woods. Brother Wo doesn't want to be near the road in case the bandits are following.

In the morning, Brother Wo insists that you both stay hidden in the woods. But later in the day, he decides that things look quiet enough to return to the road. He tells you that he can get you home shortly after nightfall.

Out on the road, you're both shocked when a different band of bandits jumps out at you. They shout, "Your money or your life!"

Brother Wo says, "I'm a penniless monk!"

"Then we'll take the kid for ransom!"

Brother Wo leaps in front of you, blocking them with his staff. He yells for you to run into the woods.

50

TURN TO PAGE 55.

A COUPLE OF DAYS LATER, YOU REACH THE TOWN. YOU FIND A GOOD SPOT TO CHECK OUT THE JAIL.

IT'S SO ANNOYING THAT HE'S RIGHT UNDER THE BREAK ROOM.

AIYAA, LI KUI THE BLACK WHIRLWIND SURE IS NOISY.

AT LEAST HE'LL BE EXECUTED SOON.

YOU REPORT IN TO THE BANDITS THAT NIGHT, AND MAHJEUK MAKES A PLAN TO BREAK INTO THE JAIL THE NEXT NIGHT.

STAY HERE AND WATCH OUR ESCAPE ROUTE.

CRASH THUMP

I'LL TEACH YOU JERKS TO LOCK ME UP!

PLEASE, LI KUI, SIR, WE MUST GO!

GO ON TO THE NEXT PAGE.

As soon as the bandits start coming over the wall, you run back through the alley to check the escape route. You hear the bandits catching up to you, and a sudden roar nearly deafens you.

"That little rat's going to report us! I'll kill it!"

You risk a glance back and see a wild-eyed, shirtless man charging at you with two battle-axes. You run for your life. The bandits have to grab him and shout an explanation until he understands that you're with them.

You can't believe this maniac is Li Kui and that you helped rescue him. Li Kui thinks that you're shifty-looking, but he agrees to bring the bandits to Liangshan Marsh.

After a few days, you arrive at a tavern by the water. Li Kui introduces all of you to Zhu Gui, known as the Dry-Land Crocodile.

Zhu Gui says, "Good timing. Marshal Gao is leading an imperial army to destroy the outlaws of Liangshan Marsh. We can use more fighters."

Li Kui boasts that he's the only fighter anyone needs.

GO ON TO THE NEXT PAGE.

TWISTED JOURNEYS®

Zhu Gui suggests that a battlefield might not be the right place for a child.

WILL YOU . . .

. . . leave before the imperial troops arrive?
TURN TO PAGE 79.

. . . stay and meet the famous Liangshan Marsh outlaws?
TURN TO PAGE 62.

You say to the monk, "Excuse me, sir?"

He looks down at you, raising one of his very long and impressive eyebrows.

"May I travel with you and learn kung fu?"

"What do your parents have to say about your leaving home?" he asks sternly, thumping his staff against the ground.

You boldly declare, "I'm an orphan!"

You wish you'd been a little quieter when the tea shop owner shouts, "That's the apothecary's kid!" *Uh-oh*.

The monk looks disgusted. "I have no use for liars." Shaking his head, he walks away.

Even worse, the tea shop owner marches you home and tells your parents that you tried to run away.

Your mother asks, "Have we been so terrible to you?" and bursts into tears. You realize that you've really hurt her feelings.

Your father is so angry, he says, "You're too irresponsible for kung fu training. Your *batgua kuen* lessons are over."

Your adventures have ended before they even began.

THE END

You think you hear running water nearby, but you're exhausted.

WILL YOU . . .

. . . find the water and follow it for a while?

TURN TO PAGE 77.

. . . just yell for help in case Brother Wo or anyone else is nearby?

TURN TO PAGE 31.

You tell Sun Simjam, "I got a little lost," and give her your best confused look.

"I'll take you," she says and leads you back to the moon-viewing pavilion.

You go to Fa May and quietly explain what you saw. She exclaims, "That can't be right!" The others look at the two of you in surprise, and Fa May repeats your story.

You're worried that you may have offended them, but Fa May is the only one who looks shocked. One or two of the others look at Wu Waanfo expectantly.

Wu Waanfo says, "Unfortunately, Saamgo has been behaving strangely. I didn't want to believe that he'd betray us, but we've suspected that he's in league with the

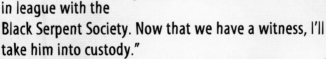

Black Serpent Society. Now that we have a witness, I'll take him into custody."

Saamgo gets caught with the poison in the guards' pantry and is locked up. Wu Waanfo orders the guards to be doubled. Any attackers will see that and know their plan was discovered.

GO ON TO THE NEXT PAGE.

WITH THEIR EVIL PLAN UNCOVERED, THE BLACK SERPENT SOCIETY ARE UNABLE TO STOP THE DUEL. TWO DAYS LATER, THE DUEL TAKES APLACE AT A TAOIST MONASTERY BEFORE A LARGE AUDIENCE OF *GONGWU* WARRIORS.

BEGIN!

DUHKSEH IS AGGRESSIVE...

...BUT FA MAY DODGES ALL HIS ATTACKS!

NNGH!

Fa May has won! You start to cheer and realize that all the shouting and yelling during the duel has faded to silence.

The audience of martial artists is bowing respectfully to Fa May. She bows back and asks them to honour the memory of her sister.

You walk with the rest of the Shining Hawk Association to join her. The audience members turn their backs on the Black Serpent Society and follow your group out of the monastery.

"*Sifu*, what will happen to them?" you ask.

Fa May says, "They have been rejected by the *gongwu* brethren. They will have to leave Wudang Mountain."

Someone asks, "Is that the child who uncovered their plot?"

"Yes," Fa May answers. "My student here saved us."

You see the warriors nodding to one another. Many praise you before leaving.

You've been accepted by the *gongwu* brethren. You've only just begun your training, but you vow to become an honourable warrior worthy of the Shining Hawk Association.

THE END

"Actually, my parents are apothecaries back home," you say.

Juklaam sneers. "Oh, another spoiled brat." He walks off with his friends, but Noiheung stays.

Gasi asks, "Don't apothecaries usually practice kung fu for health?"

You say, "My father knows *batgua kuen*."

Gasi rolls his eyes and says, "No wonder you couldn't fight the bandits. That's just breathing and defensive stuff. Shaolin *kuen* is much more powerful."

You protest that *batgua kuen* isn't just defensive. You've seen your father fight in friendly matches.

"His friends probably go easy on him," says Gasi.

It's annoying that Gasi keeps putting down *batgua kuen*. You ran away from home because your father wouldn't teach you, not because it's a weak style of fighting.

Gasi says, "Since you have no training in Shaolin *kuen*, you'll have to practice a lot to catch up. You'll have to forget *batgua kuen*."

You hadn't thought about that. In defending your father, you realize that you miss your parents. You're not sure that you want to give up *batgua kuen*.

GO ON TO THE NEXT PAGE.

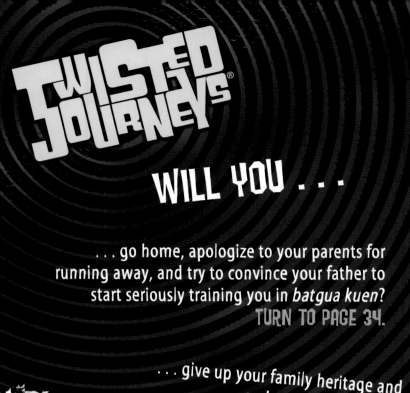

TWISTED JOURNEYS®

WILL YOU . . .

. . . go home, apologize to your parents for running away, and try to convince your father to start seriously training you in *batgua kuen*?

TURN TO PAGE 34.

. . . give up your family heritage and embrace Shaolin *kuen*?

TURN TO PAGE 93.

At the mention of imperial soldiers, Song Jiang says, "We were just putting the finishing touches on our strategy." He asks Li Kui to introduce the bandits to the other outlaws, and Li Kui puffs up in pride.

Song Jiang notices you and says, "Would you like to help out as my page? One of our generals borrowed mine."

You agree, glad to get away from Li Kui. After Li Kui and the bandits leave, Song Jiang and the others lean back over the table.

They talk about how someone named Sun the Witch and her husband sabotaged the imperial shipyards to delay their attack. Even so, Marshal Gao now has 130,000 soldiers and a fleet of more than three hundred paddleboats.

Wu Yong's strategy is to lure them deep into Liangshan Marsh and then damage their boats and trap them there. The outlaws have a lot of good swimmers who can attack the boats underwater.

GO ON TO THE NEXT PAGE.

Song Jiang says that you can stay with him on the command boat or help a general create a diversion with some other kids.

WILL YOU . . .

. . . stay with Song Jiang?
TURN TO PAGE 14.

. . . join the other kids?
TURN TO PAGE 87.

The bandits tie you up and take you back to their mountain camp. They get the ransom money from your parents pretty quickly. You've had enough adventure and look forward to going home.

Just when you think the bandits are going to take you home, one of them says, "What if the kid leads the authorities here? That brat saw our camp." They all scowl at you.

You nervously protest, "I won't say anything!"

They don't believe you. Since they already have the ransom money, they don't need you anymore. A particularly mean-looking bandit carries you farther up the mountain. You plead with him to spare your life, but he just ignores you.

He arrives at a crevice so deep that the bottom is as dark as night. With a sneer, he easily tosses you over the edge like a bag of rubbish.

THE END

You run and catch up with the woman. She seems amused when you ask to be her student and agrees to let you travel with her. She says, "My name is Fa May. You will call me *sifu*, to show me respect as your teacher."

"Yes, *sifu*," you reply. "Where are we going?"

"To Wudang Mountain. I'm meeting someone for a duel."

You can't believe your luck! Wudang Mountain is famous for all the kung fu masters who live and train there. You'll even see a duel!

The two of you walk on the road until the sun sets. You help gather firewood for camp, and Fa May shares some bread and beef jerky for dinner. She gives you an extra blanket for your bed and goes to sleep.

As you fall asleep under the stars, you realize with a thrill that you're pretty far from home now.

Fa May wakes you early, when the sky is still partly grey. You break camp and hit the road.

GO ON TO THE NEXT PAGE.

TWISTED JOURNEYS®

That bandit is obviously a coward for attacking a kid, but he's still bigger and stronger than you.

WILL YOU . . .

. . . try to use your father's training and fight back?
TURN TO PAGE 41.

. . . yell for help from Fa May?
TURN TO PAGE 19.

"I appreciate everything you've done for me, *sifu*, but I don't want to take sides yet," you answer.

Fa May looks disappointed but says, "That's probably the safe thing to do. I'll take you to the hermit Lo Yahnsih." She leads you a long way, taking you on paths sometimes barely wide enough to walk on and up steep mountainsides. You soon have no idea where you are.

You reach a cave entrance partially hidden by a giant rock. A voice calls, "Fa May! How good to see you!" You look up and see a skinny old man standing on a cliff far above.

Suddenly he leaps off the cliff, and you gasp in shock. Instead of falling to his death, however, he spins a few times as he drops and lands gently before you.

Fa May explains, "Lo Yahnsih is a master of *hing kung*, or light-body kung fu. He can leap back up just as easily."

Fa May and the hermit bow in greeting to each other.

GO ON TO THE NEXT PAGE.

In a serious tone, Fa May adds, "Lo Yahnsih is also skilled at *dimmak*."

The hermit's hands move faster than you can see as he taps a few points on your body. You can't move your arms or legs! He has used *dimmak* on *you*!

You struggle to move, but you are paralyzed. You say, "*Sifu*, why are you doing this?"

"As my student, you should be absolutely loyal to me," she explains. "Your suspicious behaviour means Lo Yahnsih will have to keep you here until after the duel."

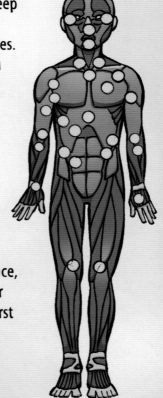

Bowing to the hermit, she leaves. He is not unkind. He releases you for meals and relieving yourself, but he is a careful guard.

You're beginning to wonder if you'll be a prisoner forever, then Fa May returns.

Lo Yahnsih releases you, and you drop to your knees, saying, "*Sifu*, I've learned my lesson! Please continue to teach me!"

Fa May gives you another chance, and you spend many years as her student. You never forget your first lesson in the rules of *gongwu*.

THE END

You step back outside and take deep gulps of air that doesn't smell like *geungsi*. Those *geungsi* really give you the creeps.

Wahnsyu says, "You didn't have to run out like that. They weren't doing anything."

"If I wait for them to do something, it'll be too late," you retort.

Wahnsyu waves dismissively and says, "They can't see. They can only detect the living by their breathing. Hold your breath, and they'll hop right past you."

You don't find this reassuring. The sun's going to set soon, and you can't wait to get far away from the *geungsi*.

Wahnsyu seems like a nice guy, but anyone who hangs out with dead people is just plain weird. You say, "It's been nice meeting you, but my parents are expecting me. I should get home."

Wahnsyu says, "Let me bolt the door, and I'll see you off."

He turns to bolt the door—and that's when you both hear a noise inside the shed.

WILL YOU . . .

. . . follow Wahnsyu in to see what made the noise?
TURN TO PAGE 18.

. . . decide that it's probably just the cat you saw earlier?
TURN TO PAGE 7.

. . . run home and get away from the *geungsi*?
TURN TO PAGE 106.

Wu Waanfo invites you to his reception room. There are shelves with jade figurines, books, and weapons. He has a servant set a meal on a table carved with mountain scenes. You sit on a matching round stool.

As you eat, Wu Waanfo tells you about Fa May's sister.

"She was beautiful and a great kung fu master. A man named Duhkseh wanted to marry her, but she refused him because he was from the villainous Black Serpent Society. One day, when she went for a walk, she was attacked by many snakes and died. Her sword, the Hawk Wing Sabre, was shattered. It was obvious that Duhkseh set the snakes on her."

You say, "*Sifu* is so cheerful that I had no idea something so terrible happened."

Wu Waanfo smiles. "I'm glad to hear Fa May's happy spirit has survived."

But you remember how upset she looked when she walked away. "I hope she's all right."

"The others are keeping an eye on her, but we can go find her if you like."

WILL YOU . . .

. . . follow Saamgo and see what he's up to?
TURN TO PAGE 16.

. . . stay and not worry about it? It's none of your business.
TURN TO PAGE 35.

You stumble toward the sound of running water. The sound is definitely louder in one direction.

You're pretty thirsty, so you hurry toward the creek or river or whatever it is. You soon see moonlight reflecting off the water.

You step eagerly toward it, only to have the ground crumble under your feet. You tumble down the bank into the river with a splash!

The water's cold, but you don't care. You gulp handfuls of it to relieve your thirst. When you wade back to the riverbank, your soaked clothes are freezing.

You have no choice but to stay in them as you trudge along the river, hoping to see some sign of people. Finally, near dawn, you find a road. In fact, you know the road—it leads to your town!

When you finally see your parents' apothecary shop, it looks like the best place in the world. You realize what a nice, safe life an apothecary enjoys, and you vow never to leave again!

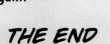

THE END

Li Kui's eyes flash when you decide to leave, and he bellows, "Since you helped rescue me, I insist on being your guard!"

Your heart sinks, and you tell him that you can manage on your own. He accuses you of holding a grudge. You're forced to give in so he won't get angrier.

He declares, "It's decided. I'll get our little friend taken care of and be back lickety-split!"

Throwing an arm around your shoulders, he rushes you out of the tavern. You can't believe you're stuck with this oaf!

After walking a few hours, Li Kui says, "It doesn't sit right with me."

You don't bother answering, since he's been talking to himself for a while, but he yells, "Hey, kid, you deaf?"

You apologize, and he says, "It's wrong to abandon your comrades before a big battle."

You turn to answer and see that he's swinging his battle-axes around. You run, but he catches up and takes care of you . . . just like he promised.

THE END

Stifling another yawn, you say, "I'd like to rest, please, Sister Gau."

The young nun gasps. "You should call her *sifu*! Have you no respect?"

Sister Gau laughs. "The child is new, sister. It's all right." She takes you to your room and tells you that someone will wake you in a few hours. You crawl under the blanket and fall asleep.

You're suddenly awakened by a sharp pain. A monk shakes you and yanks you out of bed.

He yells, "Lazy brat! How dare you hide away and sleep?" He hits you with a switch, and you realize that what woke you was the first hit of the switch. It hurts!

You say, "I'm not hiding!"

"No back talk!" He jerks you to your feet and hits you again! You start to protest, but he raises the switch as soon as you open your mouth. Better stay silent.

With a painful grip on your arm, he drags you stumbling out of your room.

GO ON TO THE NEXT PAGE.

You bow quickly to the warriors and chase Fa May into the mansion. The entrance hall has many wooden chairs with side tables. Silk tapestries hang on the walls, and curtains flutter in the doorways to other rooms. You follow Fa May through the mansion to a courtyard with a peaceful garden and a goldfish pond.

You ask, "*Sifu*, are you all right?"

She nods and says, "Of course. It's just that everything is finally almost over."

Fa May sits cross-legged on the edge of the pond and rests her chin on her fist. She says, "My sister was my best friend. When I found out that Duhkseh of the Black Serpent Society killed her, I challenged him to a duel in public so that he was forced to accept. Then I went on a secret mission to get her sword, the Hawk Wing Sabre, repaired."

You look at her sword, realizing that the plain leather wrapped around the hilt is a disguise to hide its identity!

The snake looks really dangerous, but it could bite Fa May again if you leave her.

WILL YOU . . .

. . . run to get help?
TURN TO PAGE 49.

. . . risk getting near the snake to grab the Hawk Wing Sabre and attack?
TURN TO PAGE 103.

You thank Mistress Sun for her kind offer but say that you can pay for food and lodgings. She smiles and seats you at a table.

When she brings you tea and asks for your order, you request the dumplings. Mistress Sun apologizes and says, "I'm afraid we're out. I'll have more tomorrow."

You're disappointed, but you order some rice with steamed chicken instead. Since the inn isn't near any town, you're soon the only customer there.

Mistress Sun brings you a sweet dessert drink. You finish it and get up, but it's hard to move, and you fall down.

Mistress Sun smiles as you struggle to stand. A man—he must be Mistress Sun's husband— joins her and says, "So that's the rich kid too good for honest work."

The dessert was drugged! Mistress Sun takes the bag of silver from your belt, and her husband picks up your paralyzed body.

Still smiling, she says, "Now we have silver and meat for our dumplings. Didn't I promise to have dumplings tomorrow?"

THE END

Since the bandits don't dare come into town, you're finally safe! You ask for directions to the police headquarters and hurry over there.

You find the sheriff and tell him that the Leaping Deer Mountain bandits plan to rescue the outlaw Li Kui. Alarmed, he questions you closely on where the bandits are hiding.

The sheriff collects a group of deputies and soldiers to arrest the bandits. To be safe, he sends Li Kui in a caged cart to a jail in a neighbouring town.

You lead the sheriff and his force to the meeting spot in the woods, but the bandits are gone! One of the sheriff's men finds a note stuck to a tree.

It says, "We never trusted the little snake. By now, we've freed Li Kui and have all escaped!"

The sheriff is furious and blames you for Li Kui's escape. You protest, but he shows no mercy for someone who was working with bandits.

He decides someone needs to take Li Kui's place—and that person is you!

THE END

THE PLAN WORKS, AND THE NAVY SAILS FOR THE SHORE...

...WHERE THEY ARE SURROUNDED.

EPILOGUE: THE OUTLAWS DEFEAT MARSHAL GAO. THE EMPEROR IS IMPRESSED BY THEIR BRAVERY AND OFFERS PARDONS TO THE OUTLAWS IF THEY SERVE THE EMPIRE AS ELITE TROOPS. SONG JIANG INVITES YOU TO STAY AS HIS AIDE. DEEPLY HONOURED, YOU JOIN HIM FOR A LONG AND SUCCESSFUL CAREER IN THE IMPERIAL ARMY.

You hold up your hands and say, "Look, I ran away from home to learn kung fu. So my parents are alive, but they don't really matter here."

Gasi looks shocked. He says, "I can't believe you ran away from home. Why wouldn't they let you learn kung fu?"

"My father thought I wasn't ready," you reply.

Juklaam asks what *kuen* your father practices. Although *kuen* literally means "fist," it also means "kung fu style." You tell Juklaam that your father practices *batgua kuen*.

He waves in dismissal and says, "*Batgua kuen* isn't as good as Shaolin *kuen* anyway."

Noiheung says, "The style doesn't matter as much as experience. A *batgua* master can defeat a Shaolin student."

You gloomily say, "Well, I have almost no training, so I'm not defeating anyone."

To your surprise, Gasi immediately offers to tutor you, and so does Juklaam. They seem to have forgotten their feud so they can help you out.

89

GO ON TO THE NEXT PAGE.

Wu Waanfo says, "We're pleased to have you join us." Then, his expression serious, he says to Fa May, "I suppose you're here for the reckless duel."

Fa May snaps, "You can't talk me out of it!"

As they argue, you realize that you've been caught up in the excitement of seeing a duel. You haven't thought about how Fa May could get hurt. In fact, you don't really know anything about the duel at all.

You ask, "*Sifu*, why are you fighting the duel? And who are you fighting?"

Fa May and Wu Waanfo stop arguing and look at you. Fa May bows her head for a moment and says, "I'm going to fight the person responsible for my sister's death." It's a shock to see such a sad expression on your cheerful *sifu*'s face.

"I'm sorry," you say. Fa May just walks away wiping her eyes.

Though Wu Waanfo was angry with Fa May a moment ago, he looks worried now. He says, "It's a sad story, but one you should know."

GO ON TO THE NEXT PAGE. **91**

You want to hear the full story,
but you're also worried about Fa May.

WILL YOU . . .

. . . stay and listen to Wu Waanfo?
TURN TO PAGE 74.

. . . chase after Fa May and see how she's doing?
TURN TO PAGE 82.

You shrug and say, "Let's not argue about it anymore. You're right. I've made my choice."

You get used to life at the training school pretty fast. You wake up before dawn and practice for several hours before your first meal. Afternoons would normally be a mix of meditation and Buddhism studies . . . and more practice. Now, with the demonstration coming up, everyone spends all day practising.

You become good friends with the merchant kids and Noiheung, who gets along with everyone.

But the demonstration is cancelled when *Sifu* Mohdihkge finds a student somewhere else. Although the others are disappointed, you know you are too new to stand a chance in a competition like that anyway.

You spend many years at the school, until you leave with Gasi to take charge of security for his family's business.

One day, you escort some wagons near your old hometown and decide to go visit. You're surprised to discover that it's turned into a ghost town. Some buildings are burned-out shells.

Although you investigate, you never do learn what happened to your parents.

THE END

GO ON TO THE NEXT PAGE.

You pick up the cat and rush it out of the shed while Wahnsyu checks on the other *geungsi*. You carefully close the door behind you before releasing the cat.

When Wahnsyu comes out, he says, "The *geungsi* are fine now. You did a good job. Thank you."

Wahnsyu notices that it's grown dark and decides to escort you home after setting some magical seals on the shed door.

Your mother is waiting outside your house with a lantern and cries out, "Where have you been?"

Wahnsyu bows deeply, apologizes for keeping you, and explains the situation. You're embarrassed at what a hero he says you are, but your mother seems pleased.

She invites Wahnsyu to stay for dinner, but he says he needs to return to his clients. Your mother tells your father the story over dinner, and he nods in approval.

He says, "I suppose you should learn to defend yourself properly. Can you get up at dawn for training?"

You eagerly agree, silently thanking the *geungsi*.

THE END

A loud crash wakes you up. You hear a lot of people running into the inn, and a couple of sheriff's deputies storm into your room.

One of them yells, "We got one!" and they toss you onto the floor and tie you up.

You ask what's going on, but they just march you downstairs. The inn is cleared out. All the valuables are gone. Mistress Sun and Zhang Qing must have run away during the night!

The sheriff says, "We know you people have been murdering travellers for their money. We know you get rid of the bodies by turning them into dumplings and grinding the bones into fertilizer. You'd better tell us where your friends are!"

You protest that you only got there yesterday, but they put you in jail anyway. Witnesses report that you worked in the garden, hiding evidence.

You're tattooed with the mark of a criminal on your cheek and exiled to the western provinces, never to see your home again.

THE END

TWISTED JOURNEYS®

You're still stinging from Brother Syun's switch, but you could end up in big trouble if he gets injured.

WILL YOU PICK . . .

. . . the plan to spread slippery oil outside his door?
TURN TO PAGE 110.

. . . the plan to fill his room with chickens?
TURN TO PAGE 102.

As the bell warns the town of danger, a couple of guards from the bell tower run back with you to your parents. You're relieved to find your parents safe! They'd driven off the *geungsi* with the sticky rice and torches.

The guards escort your family back to the tower. Everyone stays awake for the rest of the night. At dawn, Wahnsyu comes to the tower.

Wahnsyu bows deeply and says, "My deepest apologies for losing control of my clients. It's a good thing that the warning bell was rung. I was able to contain the *geungsi* before they injured anyone."

A guard says, "It was this brave family who warned us. They're the heroes who saved the town."

Your father tells you, "I realized last night that I should train you properly. I'm very proud of you."

You want to start right away. Your father laughs and suggests getting some sleep first. You agree, though you're not sure you *can* sleep—you're so excited. Tomorrow you'll be learning kung fu at last.

THE END

Since you don't know how much it'll cost to get home, you agree to work. Mistress Sun thanks you and takes you to the garden.

She introduces you to her husband, Zhang Qing, and goes back inside. He thanks you for helping.

Zhang Qing says, "Why don't you spread the bonemeal fertilizer, and I'll work it into the soil."

It's tough work to carry the heavy bag of fertilizer and bend over to spread it. But you finish the entire garden by dark.

Zhang Qing is pleased and tells his wife to make something special for dinner. The customers are all gone, so the three of you sit down to a feast of slow-cooked soup, roast duck, fresh vegetables, spicy beef stew, and steamed fish.

You're pretty tired, so Mistress Sun shows you to the guest room right after dinner. You fall deeply asleep but wake up in the middle of the night. Even though it's very late, there's a dim light coming through the floorboards.

GO ON TO THE NEXT PAGE.

TWISTED JOURNEYS®

You hear voices.

WILL YOU . . .

. . . go back to sleep?
TURN TO PAGE 96.

. . . sneak down and see
what's going on?
TURN TO PAGE 111.

YOU MAKE YOUR MOVE THE NEXT MORNING DURING BREAKFAST WHEN EVERYONE'S AWAY FROM THEIR ROOMS.

AHEM.

I HOPE THIS IS THE LAST TIME YOU DO THIS.

YES, SIFU.

IT'S UPSETTING THE CHICKENS.

YES, SIFU.

WITH TWO GREAT FRIENDS LIKE YUHKTIN AND CHUNGMING, YOU THINK LIFE WILL BE PRETTY GOOD HERE.

THE END

You decide that there's no time to get help or look for another weapon. You need to save Fa May now—even if it means getting near the snake to grab the Hawk Wing Sabre.

You dash forward and reach for the sword. You close your fingers around the hilt and start to jump back when the snake hisses and darts at you!

You try to dodge, but the snake is too fast. You see the snake's jaws clamp onto your arm and then you suddenly feel very dizzy. The sword drops out of your hand, and you fall paralysed on the ground.

As the world goes dark, you see a man pick up the snake. It doesn't attack him. It just wraps around his shoulders. This must be Duhkseh. He smiles at you and Fa May, knowing that he is victorious. His evil smile is the last thing you ever see.

THE END

104

You run out of the shed into the fading twilight and straight back to town.

Your father is waiting for you with a lantern in front of your house.

He cries out, "Where have you been?" He grabs your injured arm, and you yell in pain. Surprised, he pulls your sleeve back and exclaims, *"Aiyaa!"*

He doesn't ask any more questions, just hurries you inside. You've never been happier that your parents are apothecaries, as they quickly make a poultice for your arm. The warm bundle of herbal paste soothes your pain.

Your mother gives you medicine to drink with dinner. It makes you sleepy, and your father carries you to bed. You sleep all through the next day.

As the sun sets, you stop breathing. You feel very hungry and very cold. You hear someone approaching, and you rise, attracted to the warm breath of a living person.

Someone opens your bedroom door . . . and you hop toward your first victim.

THE END

Wahnsyu may be fine with *geungsi*, but you're not. You prudently turn tail and run for home. You can't get away from them fast enough.

You soon regret having gone up the hill. When the sun sets, you're still on the empty road. You run past the closed roadside tea stand, wishing you'd stuck with your plan to have a snack.

You get a pretty painful stitch in your side and slow down when you see the edge of town up ahead. Then you think you hear a faint rhythmic thumping noise behind you.

Didn't the Taoist priest say the *geungsi* hop? They must've escaped and are following you!

Your stitch forgotten, you race home. You see your father waiting for you with a lantern outside. You hurry him inside and lock the door.

You say, "The Taoist priest lost control of his *geungsi*!"

You expected to have to convince your parents, but your father just nods and hurries to find your mother. It's weird, but they seem to know exactly what to do.

106

GO ON TO THE NEXT PAGE.

STICKY RICE BURNS *GEUNGSI* IF THEY STEP ON IT. WE'LL PUT SOME BY ALL THE DOORS AND WINDOWS.

JUST GRAB ANY CHICKEN. WE NEED TO BE QUICK.

GO GET INK AND A BIG SPOOL OF THREAD.

CHICKEN-BLOOD INK ALSO BURNS THEM.

IT'S AS BRIGHT AS WE CAN MAKE IT. IF THEY GET THIS FAR INSIDE, THE LIGHT MAY DRIVE THEM OFF.

I'M WORRIED ABOUT THE REST OF THE TOWN.

GO ON TO THE NEXT PAGE.

You don't want to go outside now that you're safe, but no one else in town even knows about the *geungsi*!

DO YOU . . .

. . . agree with your father that people need to be warned?
TURN TO PAGE 98.

. . . convince your father to stay here where it's safe?
TURN TO PAGE 25.

You aren't lying much when you tell Brother Wo that you don't remember which direction you came from. He drags you around for a while asking if anything looks familiar.

You tell him everything looks the same in the dark. Brother Wo finally gives up and lets you go to sleep.

When you open your eyes in the morning, you see a giant face looming over you and you yell out in fright. The face jerks back, and you realize that it's Brother Wo.

Stroking his beard, Brother Wo says, "I think the *sehjing* cast a spell on you. She may try to get you to come to her. Your parents will have to make sure from now on that you don't go out at night."

All you want is to get home. When you finally do, your parents are overjoyed and gather you up in a big hug.

Unfortunately, they believe Brother Wo and hire a guard to follow you around all the time. You can never have privacy again.

THE END

Yuhktin grins in approval. Chungming protests half-heartedly but seems resigned.

You're so excited that you wake right up when Yuhktin scratches at your door that night. Chungming is with her. The three of you sneak to Rat Whiskers' room and pour the oil so that he won't be able to leave his room without stepping in it.

The next morning, you're having breakfast together in the dining hall when a monk runs in calling for the doctor. He says that Brother Syun has broken his arm. Yuhktin gasps and looks scared.

A little later, a very angry Sister Gau tells the three of you that she knows you poured the oil. You're all expelled and have to pack your things and go home.

Your escorts allow you to say farewell to one another at the gates.

"I'm sorry. This is my fault," says Yuhktin.

You say, "We're equally responsible." Chungming agrees.

Before parting, you make a pact to remain friends and reunite some day under better circumstances.

THE END

WHICH TWISTED JOURNEYS®

WILL YOU TRY NEXT?

#1 CAPTURED BY PIRATES
Can you keep a band of scurvy pirates from turning you into shark bait?

#2 ESCAPE FROM PYRAMID X
Not every ancient mummy stays dead . . .

#3 TERROR IN GHOST MANSION
The spooks in this Halloween house aren't wearing costumes . . .

#4 THE TREASURE OF MOUNT FATE
Can you survive monsters and magic and bring home the treasure?

#5 NIGHTMARE ON ZOMBIE ISLAND
Will you be the first to escape Zombie Island?

#6 THE TIME TRAVEL TRAP
Danger is everywhere when you're caught in a time machine!

#7 VAMPIRE HUNT
Vampire hunters are creeping through an ancient castle. And you're the vampire they're hunting!

#8 ALIEN INCIDENT ON PLANET J
Make peace with the Makaknuk, Zirifubi, and Frongo, or you'll never get off their planet . . .

#9 AGENT MONGOOSE AND THE HYPNO-BEAM SCHEME
Your top-secret mission, if you choose to accept it: foil the plots of an evil mastermind!

#10 THE GOBLIN KING
Will you join the fearsome goblins or the dangerous elves?

#11 SHIPWRECKED ON MAD ISLAND
Mad scientists and mutants are on your trail! Will you escape them . . . or join them?

#12 KUNG FU MASTERS
Take the challenge to fight bandits and ghosts, and become a master of martial arts!

This book was first published in the United States of America in 2009.
Copyright © 2009 by Lerner Publishing Group, Inc.